IMAGES
of America

PAUL SMITH'S ADIRONDACK
HOTEL AND COLLEGE

Paul Smith (signature)

Apollos Austin (Paul) Smith was born in Vermont but gained wealth and fame in the Adirondack Mountains of New York. He started with a small country inn and ended up owning one of the most famous resorts in 19th-century America, large tracts of forestland, a railroad, power and telephone companies, and other businesses. With all of this, his peers might best remember him as a great storyteller. Today his name lives on through Paul Smith's College, the College of the Adirondacks, his adopted home. (Courtesy of Paul Smith's College of Arts and Sciences.)

On the cover: Please see page 29. (Courtesy of Paul Smith's College of Arts and Sciences.)

IMAGES
of America

PAUL SMITH'S ADIRONDACK HOTEL AND COLLEGE

Neil Surprenant

ARCADIA
PUBLISHING

Published by Arcadia Publishing
Charleston, South Carolina

Printed in the United States of America

Library of Congress Control Number: 2008930180

For all general information contact Arcadia Publishing at:
Telephone 843-853-2070
Fax 843-853-0044
E-mail sales@arcadiapublishing.com
For customer service and orders:
Toll-Free 1-888-313-2665

Visit us on the Internet at www.arcadiapublishing.com

To Randy Lewis, *the real writer in the family*

CONTENTS

ACKNOWLEDGMENTS

Many people deserve thanks for their help in putting this book together. Mike Beccaria, systems librarian at Paul Smith's College, provided valuable technical expertise in the compiling of this material. Bob Seidenstein and Kirk Peterson provided help identifying people in pictures from the early days of the college. Tom Smith deserves thanks for his work scanning images. Finally, whenever I think I have a good handle on the history of Paul Smith's Hotel or College, I spend a little time with Prof. Emeritus Gould Hoyt and find out that, compared to him, I know nothing. Thank you to him for many of the best stories that give life to people who are long gone.

This book would not have been possible with the photographs provided by Paul Smith's College. With the exception of one image provided by Prof. Randall Swanson, all images are courtesy of Paul Smith's College.

INTRODUCTION

Apollos Austin (Paul) Smith was born in Milton, Vermont, in 1825. He was expected to work in the family lumber and sawmill business, but there was a problem with this: he was not interested. He left home at about the age of 16 and got a job on the canal boats that ran north and south through the lakes and canals between Albany and Montreal, Quebec, in Canada. When the waterways froze every winter, Smith was forced to return to logging. By his early 20s, he came up with a way to avoid that life completely. When the canal season ended, he traveled into the western mountains, the Adirondacks, to hunt, fish, and trap. This was a way to supplement the family income without having to log or work in the mill at all. It did not take Smith long to realize that he liked the hunting and fishing a lot more than he even liked working on the canal boats.

Smith decided that the best job he could get would be to turn his passion for the outdoors into his living. He convinced his family that their future was in the Adirondacks. They sold the business and moved to Loon Lake. There they opened a rough country inn called Hunter's Home. Smith's mother did the cooking and cleaning. His father raised animals and a garden to feed their guests. Smith's job was to guide the men who came to stay at Hunter's Home on hunting and fishing trips through the Adirondack wilderness. The family prospered in their new life.

Hunter's Home had one large bunk room on the second floor where the men slept in their bedrolls. It was only for men because it would have been inappropriate for men and women to share quarters in those days. Dr. Hezekiah Loomis from Boston was a frequent guest.

Loomis wanted to bring his family to the mountains, and he was so impressed by the job young Smith did running Hunter's Home that he offered him money to buy or build a new inn as long as it would accommodate women and children. Smith took Loomis to a spot on the shores of Lower St. Regis Lake in Franklin County that he knew was for sale. They agreed that the location was perfect. Smith purchased the land and started construction on a new hostelry in the summer of 1858.

While Smith was building his hotel in 1858, he was also courting Lydia Helen Martin of Franklin Falls. She was born in AuSable Forks on August 29, 1834. She and Smith met at a dance near Loon Lake. After dancing the waltz all evening, their courtship began. They were married on May 5, 1859. They did not enjoy much of a honeymoon because their new 17-room hotel, at first called the St. Regis Lake House, opened that summer, and there was a lot of work to do to get the place ready.

In the early days of the hotel, Paul guided all of the sportsmen himself. Lydia did the cooking and cleaning for their guests. There were not many places where a family could stay in the wilds of the Adirondacks at this time, so business was good from the start.

They received a real boost to their hotel from an unlikely source. The Civil War started in 1861. In 1863, the Union instituted the first draft in American history to fill the ranks of its armies. The one legal way out of this draft was for a man to pay $300 for a substitute to take his place. Many young men who paid to get out of the draft left their urban homes for the wilds of the Adirondacks and the St. Regis Lake House just to get out of sight of their neighbors. They carried word of the great food, superb hunting, cleanliness of this backwoods retreat, and the Smiths' hospitality back to the richest families in the north. After the war, this word-of-mouth advertising led to a boom in business.

By 1870, Paul and Lydia's roles changed to management as they hired more and more workers for their expanding business. While Paul ran the operations related to what would today be called guest services, Lydia used her education to take on operations. They were both entrepreneurs, but she does not get the credit she deserves in this partnership.

An example of Lydia's skills was her instigation of the renamed Paul Smith's Hotel Company's dealings in land. In 1887, she purchased 10,000 acres of land around the St. Regis chain of lakes. In 1889, 4,000 acres more were added, and $20,000 was paid for an additional 13,000 acres in 1891. She anticipated that the wealthy visitors to the hotel would be interested in owning their own waterfront lots in the mountains. She was correct, and these well-off visitors then bought those lots from the Smiths in order to build camps. The Smiths then had crews log the trees from some of the land that was not on water. The logs were then skidded to the lakes and floated to the new sawmill built by the Smiths adjacent to their hotel. They then sold lumber to build camps for the families who had just purchased land from them. Real estate and lumber sales became lucrative new additions to their expanding business empire. In some cases, the city buyers paid as much for individual 5- to 20-acre lots as Lydia paid for the original large tracts of land.

At the same time that the Smiths were building their business, they were also starting a family. They had three sons. Henry B. L. was born in 1861, Phelps was born in 1862, and Apollos Austin (Paulie) Jr. was born in 1871.

All through the later 1800s, the rich and famous of American society made Paul Smith's Hotel their home base for vacations in the Adirondack Mountains. The 1890s was a time of particularly rapid growth for the company, but it was also a time of great tragedy. The Smiths' eldest son, Henry, and Lydia both passed away in 1891.

The new century found the company, now headed by Paul and his son Phelps, involved in several new businesses. They founded a railroad as well as the first electric power and telephone companies in the region.

Paul died in 1912 of a kidney problem at the age of 87. In his 1921 book, A *History of the Adirondacks*, Alfred L. Donaldson had this to say about Paul:

> His lifetime spanned the long transition from oxen to automobile, from corduroy to macadam, from hardship to luxury. He hewed his fortune and his fame out of the primeval wilderness and he compassed the former without tarnishing the latter. He lived and died respected and loved by young and old, rich and poor alike. In the early days of his hotel, his name is said to have been more frequently printed and more frequently spoken than any other in the state. I have heard it fall from the lips of high and low for many years, but I have never heard it coupled with malice or reproach.

The funeral united people from across the social spectrum. A special train carried a large number of wealthy businessmen and their families from the cities to the snow-covered wilderness to pay homage. At the same time, the local guides, merchants, and woodsmen came in from their mountain homes, many on snowshoes, to pay last respects to their friend, one of their own who had made it big.

Phelps assumed total control of the operations of Paul Smith's Hotel and all other businesses after his father's death. The hotel continued to prosper through the second decade of the 20th century, but during the 1920s, things began to change. Changes in American society, the rise of the automobile, and new technologies all combined to decrease business at Paul Smith's Hotel and the rest of the big 19th-century Adirondack hotels. In 1929, the stock market crash really hurt business. On September 5, 1930, came the most devastating blow. The main hotel caught fire and burned to the ground in four hours.

Phelps developed grand plans for rebuilding, but the Great Depression was at its worst, and the number of guests continued to dwindle. The hotel was not even able to finish a huge reconstruction project that was started. Phelps died in 1937. With his death, however, he planted the seeds for the future economic transition of the northern Adirondacks. In his will, he left the bulk of his estate to the founding of a college. He wanted the new school to offer degrees in hotel and resort management and forestry, because the Smith family fortune was based on the family hotel and the forests of the Adirondacks. He also wanted degrees in the liberal arts to be granted. Phelps decreed that this institution be named Paul Smith's College of Arts and Sciences to honor his father.

Before this new college could open, World War II intervened. For the duration of the war, the hotel buildings were leased out to the U.S. Army Signal Corps as a training facility.

The war ended in 1945, and the college opened in the fall of 1946. The early classes were made up mostly of veterans taking advantage of the free higher education offered by the GI Bill. Their large numbers ensured the early success of the college.

As time went by, the college's program offerings changed and diversified. Surveying, recreation, culinary arts, natural resources management, ecotourism and fisheries, and wildlife sciences are just some of the degrees that were added over the years. The student body has also diversified. From its beginnings catering to mostly male war veterans from New York State, the college now brings in men and women from across America and the world.

Paul and Lydia brought an entrepreneurial spirit and drive to their new home on Lower St. Regis Lake. They used that spirit to create a nationally famous hotel and a diversified, successful company. Their son Phelps then used the business they created to endow a college that would carry their entrepreneurial spirit forward to thousands of students who would come to Paul Smiths and learn to create their own success.

One

COUNTRY INN TO GILDED AGE RESORT

His given name was Apollos Austin Smith. He was born in Milton, Vermont, in 1825. When he was a child, his family called him "Pol" for short. As he got older and moved out into the world, people heard this and thought the word was Paul, so they started to call him that. Smith went along with this and found his name changed to Paul Smith, the name he carried with him the rest of his life.

Paul Smith fell in love with the Adirondacks in his early 20s. He became a hunting and fishing guide and was such a good one that one of his clients offered to loan him the money to build his own small hotel. He found a spot on Lower St. Regis Lake and began construction in 1858.

While Smith was building his hotel in 1858, he was also courting Lydia Helen Martin of Franklin Falls. This was no easy matter since it was a good 15 miles from Smith's home to Franklin Falls. The trip was not so bad on a horse in good weather, but Smith was known to cover the distance on snowshoes through the long Adirondack winter then dance all night once he got there. They were married on May 5, 1859.

Above is Lydia's family about 1875. This was a time when women in rural areas often received very little formal education. Lydia was an exception to this. Her family sent her to the Emma Willard School for women in Troy.

Paul and Lydia's hotel opened in the summer of 1859. The original name was the St. Regis Lake House. It was a small country inn of 17 rooms. Paul was the guide who took the guests hunting and fishing. Lydia did the housekeeping and cooked meals. Above is the hotel about 1865. By this time, it had already doubled in size. The portion on the left is the original.

This picture of Paul Smith is from a stereopticon slide. Stereopticons were hand-held viewers that allowed pictures like that above to be viewed in three-dimensional form. It could be described as a primitive version of the children's Viewmaster of the 1950s and 1960s. The slides were sold to tourists in many 19th-century vacation destinations as souvenirs of their trips.

This is an 1875 view of what was by then called Paul Smith's Hotel. To the left is the original boathouse. Boats were stored on the bottom level. The second floor housed sleeping quarters for the staff of guides now employed by the hotel company. Toward the right and back of the central hotel building is an addition that was constructed a few years earlier.

These guides worked for the Paul Smith's Hotel Company about 1875. In the early days of the hotel, Smith guided all the guests himself. By the later 1860s, business had expanded so much that he had to hire other local men to take over that job. These guides took the men hunting and fishing and led the women and children on boating and picnicking parties on routes like the trip of the seven carries through what is now the St. Regis Wilderness Canoe Area.

This print shows the hotel grounds from the lake about 1877. In less than 18 years, the Smiths grew their place from one building into the complex seen here. Guests carried the word of their hospitality back to the richest families in America.

In addition to guiding, Paul Smith became the public face of the business. He became what hotel people often call the "front of the house" man. He was the greeter and the one who made sure rooms were comfortable, the guide was ready for trips into the forest, and that guests' glasses were never empty.

Lydia Smith is pictured here with their second son, Phelps. She became an excellent businesswoman and the "back of house" person. She kept the accounts, hired and fired all the housekeeping and cooking staff, supervised purchasing, and wrote the contracts that her husband executed. Lydia deserves much credit for the success of the family business. She was a true partner in the operation and a woman ahead of her time.

This is the garden of Fouquet's Hotel in Plattsburgh about 1880. Lydia found out from one of her guests that the railroad was going to extend its line to this Lake Champlain village. She purchased Fouquet's just prior to the announcement that the new Delaware and Hudson Railway station would be built right across the street from her new acquisition. This newly prosperous hotel was renamed the Fouquet House. As an apprenticeship, Phelps later managed it before he took over running Paul Smith's Hotel in the late 1890s.

This logging crew is out cutting trees for the Paul Smith's sawmill. The logs were then skidded to the lakes and floated to the new sawmill built by the Smiths adjacent to their hotel. The lumber was then sold to the big-city visitors who were buying waterfront lots from the Smiths in order to build camps on the St. Regis Lakes. Real estate and lumber sales became lucrative new additions to their business empire.

Famed British novelist Charles Dickens gave this description of Paul Smith when he was touring the United States during Smith's guiding days: "A tall athletic Yankee, with no superfluous flesh about him, rawboned, with a good-natured twinkle in his blue eyes, brimful of genuine Yankee humor: he has no bad habits, and is, withal, the best rifle shot, paddler and compounder of forest stews in the whole region."

Boating was always one of the favorite activities at the hotel. These two young men and their unsuspecting friend have decided to skip the more traditional methods of getting around on Lower St. Regis Lake by building their own raft. The good news for their parents is that the wind usually blows across the lake toward the hotel, so they would have had a hard time getting out into the lake from where this picture was taken.

In his guidebook to the Adirondacks from the late 1870s, writer and photographer Seneca Ray Stoddard gives the following description of the hotel, above, from the same time period. "Paul Smiths is a surprise to everybody; an astonishing mixture of fish and fashion, pianos and puppies, Brussels carpeting and cowhide boots. Surrounded by a dense forest; out-of-the-way of all travel save that which is its own; near the best hunting and fishing grounds it is a first-class watering place with all of the modern appliances, and a table that is seldom equaled in the best city hotels,

and it is set right down in the middle of a howling wilderness. Around the house the timid deer roam; within, they rest. Without, the noble buck crashes through the tangled forest; within, his noble namesake straddles elegantly over the billiard tables and talks horses. Out on the lake the theoretical veteran casts all manner of flies; in the parlors the contents of huge Saratoga trunks are scientifically played, and nets are spread for a different kind of fish."

Business was so good at the hotel that there were times during the peak summer season that tents had to be erected in order to handle the overflow guests. Two can be seen to the right on the lakeshore between the hotel and the boathouse. Others can be glimpsed through the trees. Many guests took to making their reservations for the next season before they even left at the end of the summer. That was one way for guests to be assured that they would not end up in a tent.

These young men are the Smith brothers, the sons of Paul and Lydia Smith. Phelps is standing, and Henry B. L. (right) and Apollos Austin (Paulie) Jr. are seated. In the early days of the hotel, there were no schools between Saranac Lake and Duane, a distance of over 30 miles. Lydia homeschooled her sons and several children of local families until the first school was started at the nearby community of Keese's Mills in 1867.

Phelps Smith, the second son of Paul and Lydia, was born on June 4, 1862. He was named after Paul's father. Phelps followed in his mother's footsteps and developed an interest in business. He was an 1881 graduate of the Eastman Business College in Poughkeepsie. At the time of his death in 1937, he was still in possession of a highly complementary letter of recommendation written for him by several of the school's faculty members when he graduated.

Paulie Smith (standing at right) was Paul and Lydia's third son. He was born on August 3, 1871. Paulie spent some time in local schools, but most of his education was at a notoriously strict military academy in Peekskill, the Trinity School. On June 8, 1886, Lydia wrote to Phelps to say that Paulie was unhappy and not doing well in his schoolwork. She asked if Phelps would join her in a visit to cheer and encourage him. Phelps agreed, they went, and shortly after, she received a letter from Paulie about his higher grades and improved attitude toward Trinity.

The most popular sport in America in the late 19th century was baseball. In order to provide an added entertainment for their guests, several of the larger Adirondack hotels started a league and hired college players and the better local boys to play for them. The teams played one another at the various hotels for the guests to watch. This picture of the Paul Smith's Hotel team includes Paulie Smith in the center of the second row.

Henry B. L. Smith was the eldest of Paul and Lydia's sons. He was born on March 4, 1861. Henry was the son who most took after his father with his love of the outdoors, hunting, and fishing. Maybe following in his father's footsteps was why he was said to have been his mother's favorite.

Chas. Derby,   Morrisonville, N. Y.

Hunting was one of the most popular guest activities from the earliest days of the hotel. The success of this group shows why. There were set fees for the various hunting and fishing trips available. One could visit the Prospect House on Upper Saranac Lake for $1 a night or Corey's or Bartlett's for $2. These prices included a guide, but he would expect a hefty tip if the hunt proved successful. One of the more popular nonhunting trips was to rent saddle horses and ride to the top of St. Regis Mountain for $1 per person.

In the summer of 1870, two Italian immigrants walked 50 miles through the woods from the closest train station with an organ and a dancing bear because they heard that P. T. Barnum was staying at the hotel. They wanted to show him their act. When they arrived, one of guides told them they had better be careful, "because people shoot bears in these parts." In spite of that warning, the trip was a success because they made money from the guests who liked their act and Barnum hired them for his circus.

By the summer of 1880, the hotel had grown to four stories and had 175 rooms. In his *Guide to the Adirondacks*, published that year, E. R. Wallace said that the hotel "is supplied with every modern convenience, including bathrooms, barbershop and billiard tables. There is an extensive livery stable and a telegraph office connected to the house, likewise a boat and guide building. . . . Tents, blankets and all of the paraphernalia required in camp life, also, every variety of the choicest supplies, including numerous delicacies, are furnished to all who wish them."

From 1859 to 1890, guests traveled from their homes by train to one of the Adirondack stations. There they were picked up by stagecoach for a ride to Paul Smith's Hotel, sometimes as long as 50 miles. By 1869, business had outgrown the local and sometimes unreliable Adirondack stagecoach system, so the hotel company purchased two Concord stagecoaches from New Hampshire and added that service for its guests. The coach was noted for using matched sets of all black or all white horses. Note the guests sitting on the rooftop seats and imagine what their ride must have been like in the open air on dirt roads in all types of weather. There is no mention in the hotel records whether they paid a discount rate for those seats.

George Meserve was a longtime stagecoach driver for the Paul Smith's Hotel coaches. He was an Adirondacker who learned to drive wagons as a member of a Union artillery regiment during the Civil War. Legend has it that Gen. William Tecumseh Sherman watched him maneuver a caisson during a battle and was so impressed with his technique and calm under fire that he made Meserve his personal driver for the rest of the war.

In the winter, one could take advantage of the frozen ground to move heavy loads in places that would be impossible the rest of the year. This sled is hauling a log in front of the hotel. From the size of the log, one can tell it is virgin timber from an old-growth forest. Old-growth forests are land areas that have not been subjected to logging and other significant activities by humans. Of the 6 million acres in the Adirondack Park in the first decade of the 21st century, it is estimated that fewer than 50,000 acres are true old growth.

The headquarters for organizing outdoor activities at any Adirondack hotel was always the boathouse. This stereopticon slide view is a scene of the people gathered on the Paul Smith's Hotel boathouse dock about 1880. Guests went to the boathouse to meet the guide for fishing or hunting trips, a picnic, or just a boat ride on the lake. As is noticeable by looking at the women to the left side, it was also a great spot to just sit, relax, and listen to the waves lap on the shore.

This is a front view of the same boathouse about 1885. Arrayed on the dock are Adirondack guide boats. These boats were folk art with a high level of practicality and were designed by the guides. In the early days, the boats were also built by the guides, often in the off-season when they were out of work. These were workboats and had to meet the very specific demands of the men who designed, built, and used them.

One of the demands placed on a guide boat was that it had to be light enough for the guide to be able to move it from one body of water to another as he led his party through the backcountry. The most common term used for the act of moving a boat is to portage it, but not in the Adirondacks. In these mountains, one carried the boat. The land over which one does this is also called a carry. In the Adirondacks, signs direct canoeists to Indian Carry or Bartlett's Carry and scores of others.

In addition to being light enough to carry over rough mountain trails, the guide boat had to be maneuverable on the rivers, stable on big lakes and small ponds, and able to carry the heavy loads of equipment and food necessary for prolonged trips into the Adirondack backcountry. This elegant craft met all of those needs and more. Even in the 21st century, with the advent of Kevlar, fiberglass, and plastic boats, the Adirondack guide boat has survived.

This is the Ricketson boat shop in Bloomingdale about 1890. Once the Adirondacks became one of the busiest vacation destinations in America after 1870, the individual guide/craftsmen could no longer keep up with the demand for guide boats from the big hotels and the visitors who built their own camps and wanted their own guide boats. This led to the rise of professional boatbuilders. Many came from the ranks of the guides themselves. Nearly every town in the Adirondacks had at least one. Many of their names are legendary. Saranac Lake had Theodore Hanmer and his son Willard as well as the father-and-son team of William A. and H. K. Martin. The tradition lives on in people like Chris Woodward of Woodward's Boat Shop, also of Saranac Lake.

This is William H. Smith (no relation). His occupation was hermit. Smith fought in the Civil War, and when he returned to his hometown of Mooers, just south of the Canadian border, he decided to drop out of society. At one point, his relatives burned him out of his house, hoping to force him to return home. He responded by moving deeper into the wilderness and building a new hut made of stone. No one knows what finally happened to him or where he rests. Only this picture survives to mark his passing.

Professional photographer Charles Derby of Morrisonville took this portrait of a group of the Paul Smith's Hotel guides about 1888. Henry B. L. Smith is here too, standing, with his foot on the chair, second from the left. Seated second from the left, in his youngest-known picture, is Ben Muncil. Muncil later became a noted camp designer and builder. At this time, his building talents were unknown, and he was just a young guide.

Also from the late 1880s comes this picture of Paulie Smith standing in front of the hotel with remnants of snow on the ground around him. Spring comes late in the mountains; in most years, the snow is not this far gone until mid-April. This is mud season. The dirt roads would have been nearly impassable because of the ground being saturated from snowmelt and the first rains. Late May was the usual opening time for the hotel.

This hunting party has just returned from a successful expedition. Guests or tourists in the 19th and early 20th centuries were called sports. Clothing was usually the biggest clue to identifying who were the sports and who were the guides. Guides did not generally wear ties. The sports almost always wore ties. That would identify the men third and fourth from the right as the sports.

Sports were not just men. This mixed-gender group is out on a hunting trip, and it has brought its photographer along. The late 1800s was the time before the invention of small, portable cameras that anyone could use. This picture was taken with a large-format view camera that required considerable expertise to take successful pictures. Note the long dresses the women are wearing. This was the style of the day, but it did not make hunting, hiking, or climbing mountains very easy. In spite of this obstacle, women took to the woods in large numbers.

Here the guides are unloading the results of the day's hunt at a semipermanent camp. One of the popular hunting methods of the 19th century was jacklighting. Guides placed a metal basket attached to a short pole on the front of their boats. The basket was filled with flammable material and lit on fire, and then the boat set out in the dark of night. The sport sat in the front of the boat behind the flaming torch with his gun at the ready. They then moved along the river as quietly as possible, hoping that when a deer came down to the river, it would be mesmerized by the light of the torch, much as deer are these days by automobile headlights. When the boat got close to the animal, the sport opened fire and bagged his quarry. Jacklighting is now illegal in New York State.

Some of the wealthy people who flocked to the mountains to visit hotels like Paul Smith's decided to build their own summer homes. From about 1870 through the 1920s, an architectural style evolved around the building of what today are called the great camps of the Adirondacks. Many of these great camps started out as collections of canvas tents spread out along the lakefronts like the ones in this 1881 picture from Upper St. Regis Lake.

This is the boathouse from Camp Wild Aire on Upper St. Regis Lake about 1885. The bark-covered walls show how natural materials were used in the rustic style of the great camps. Most of the people who built camps on the St. Regis Lakes were formerly Paul Smith's Hotel guests.

Camp Wild Aire has separate buildings for different functions instead of one large lodge. Here is the dining room building and one of the sleeping cabins. Built by *New York Herald-Tribune* publisher Whitlelaw Reid, it was called the earliest artistic camp on Upper St. Regis Lake when construction began in 1882.

This interior photograph shows one of the sleeping cabins at Camp Wild Aire in 1884. Japanese ornamental art was very popular at this time. There are several fans and other pieces in a seemingly odd combination with rustic elements like taxidermy, snowshoes, and bark-covered walls.

This guide is in charge of a set of hunting hounds. He has a belt around his waist with several chains attached to the collars of the dogs around him. The dogs were used for hounding deer. In this method of hunting, the sport was set up at a spot in the woods, and the dogs were taken a distance away with likely deer habitat in between. The dogs were then turned loose to drive the terrified deer to the waiting sport. He or she would then fire away at the deer as they ran by.

As the hotel business continued to expand in the 1880s, the Smiths began to build cottages around the grounds for guests to rent. This is Milbank Cottage. It was named after the family to whom it was regularly rented in the first years after it was built.

After Paul Smith gave up guiding, he became more involved in seeing to the comfort of his guests. One place he could be found was entertaining guests on the front porch. Here he often held court with jokes and stories. After his death, some of his legendary stories were collected into a book called *The Funny Sayings of Paul Smith* by E. Long.

The front porch was not the only place Paul Smith saw to his guests. Here he is on a boat cruise on Lower St. Regis Lake, and everyone seems to be in excellent spirits. People came back to Paul Smith's Hotel as much for the convivial atmosphere provided by the host as they did for woodland recreation. There were many hotels in the Adirondacks but only one Paul Smith's.

Guide boats were not the only option for seeing the sights on the St. Regis Lakes. Here two naphtha launches are coming out of the slough from Spitfire Lake headed back toward the hotel across the lake. Naphtha was a fuel used in early motorboats. It was highly flammable and explosive, and gasoline engines quickly replaced it when they were invented.

In 1885, P. T. Barnum and his grandson posed for this portrait during one of his many visits. Barnum and Smith were great friends. This fact led to the myth that Smith named nearby Barnum Pond in his honor. In fact, Barnum Pond was named after one of the original highway superintendents of the town of Brighton where Paul Smiths is located.

While visiting Paul Smith's Hotel on September 15, 1885, Barnum received news that one of his circus trains had been involved in an accident in St. Thomas, Ontario, Canada. He also learned the terrible news that Jumbo the elephant, the most popular animal in the history of his circus, was crushed by a locomotive. Barnum left behind this photograph of the accident scene.

Glover Cottage was built on the shores of Lower St. Regis Lake about 1890. It is another example of the rental houses built on the hotel grounds. Families who were frequent guests could have these cottages custom built to their specifications, and they got the right of first refusal on renting every season. The hotel company, however, did retain ownership.

Various photographers sold scenic pictures of the hotel and its grounds to the visitors as souvenirs. This picture, titled "St. Regis Lake from Paul Smiths," was taken by Baldwin Photos of Plattsburgh about 1890. Another of the rental cottages is visible on the hill.

The St. Regis Yacht Club Committee is posing in 1917. This group was formed to promote racing of the Idem, a type of sailboat designed exclusively for use on the St. Regis Lakes. Idems are still raced on the lakes. One is on exhibit at the Adirondack Museum in Blue Mountain Lake.

On December 12, 1890, the Paul Smith's Hotel Corporation was formed. The chairman of the board was Paul Smith. The board of directors was Lydia Smith, Henry B. L. Smith, Phelps Smith, and Paulie Smith. The establishment of the corporation aided the operation of the new enterprises the company was becoming involved in.

A naphtha launch approaches the main boathouse of Paul Smith's Hotel in 1890. The 1890s was the time of the greatest expansion for the hotel and the business in general. In between the two boathouses is the newly constructed hotel store.

This 1892 photograph of the hotel was taken from the rocks at Picnic Point. It shows that a new boathouse has been constructed since the previous year. The new boathouse was called the Casino, not for the gambling that went on, but because it was Italian for "little house." The idea was that it was an annex, a little house, compared to the big house, the main hotel building.

The Casino had storage for boats on the ground floor, but the rest of the building was completely repurposed from its predecessor. The lakeside location was deemed too valuable to have guides bunking on the second floor.

This was the men's billiard room on the second floor of the Casino. There was a second one for women and separate card rooms for men and women. It was thought to be unseemly for men and women to engage in those activities together in the Gilded Age.

This was the Grill Room in the Paul Smith's Casino. The mission-style furniture in this lakeside dining room was very popular in Adirondack camps and hotels during this period. There was also a room with a ticker tape machine tied directly to the New York Stock Exchange so the men could keep track of business while they were on vacation.

Here is the Paul Smith's Hotel store in 1905. This was a true general store. It had groceries, dry goods, sundries, and lots of penny candy. A gasoline pump was added when cars replaced horses. During Prohibition, Phelps Smith had what he called the hardware counter set up in the basement. In fact, it was a secret bar, or speakeasy, only for a few invited guests and friends.

The building boom of the 1890s included many new private camps on the St. Regis Lakes. This was good for the Smiths' sawmill business. This load of logs is waiting to be put on a train.

This is a typical summer day's crowd enjoying the lakeshore recreation next to the Casino. Their clothing dates this to around 1910. On sunny summer days, this was one of the most popular spots at the hotel for socializing. In the background is Picnic Point.

The 1890s were a time not only for business growth but also of personal tragedy for the family. Eldest son Henry B. L. Smith was stricken with pneumonia and died on January 3, 1891. In his prayer book, his mother wrote, "My precious child is gone and Mother's heart is full of sorrow." He was only 29.

Lydia Smith could not get over her son's death. She kept asking why God had taken her son and where she had failed as a mother. Her letters indicated her general good health during 1891. In a November 2 letter to her sister Lucy, she said, "We are all quite well." Three days later, she was dead. What was the cause? The family said she grieved herself to death.

Paul Smith took the two deaths hard, but the response of the 66-year-old was to bury himself in his work. One of his projects was the founding of the Paul Smith's Railroad Company. This is the new Paul Smith's station.

In 1906, the Paul Smith's Electric Railway was started. Smith is on the left showing off the electric engine that powered his railroad. This standard-gauge rail line allowed the guests to skip the rough ride in the stagecoach and come right onto the grounds of the hotel by train.

The Paul Smith's Electric Railway had a jack works, a facility for loading and unloading logs from a train, on Lower St. Regis Lake where logs were taken from its flatcars and piled up on the ice. When the lake thawed in the spring, the logs were floated down to the sawmill for processing.

Here the railroad engine sits on the hotel grounds about 1929. On the left is the store, and on the right is the main hotel. Guests who arrived by private railroad car could now bring those cars right to the hotel also.

Getting a picture taken with the grand old man of the Adirondacks became an item on the list of many early-20th-century tourists. Here Paul Smith sits with several admirers in their souvenir photograph.

This is the original St. John's in the Wilderness Episcopal Church. It was consecrated by Bishop William C. Doane of Albany on September 13, 1877. This church was destroyed by fire in the wee hours of Sunday morning, December 4, 1928.

After the fire destroyed the original church, Dr. Edward Livingston Trudeau led a fund-raising drive to build this new St. John's in the Wilderness. It was designed by architects William Distin and Arthur Wilson of Saranac Lake. This building overlooks Church Pond on Route 86 near Paul Smiths Corners.

Church at Paul Smith's, Adirondack Mts.

No. 156   Moore & Gibson Co. N. Y. Germany

The superintendent of the Adirondack Mission of the Presbyterian Church, Rev. William B. Lusk, made his headquarters at Paul Smith's Hotel in 1897. He had this church built in Keese's Mills overlooking the St. Regis River in 1899. It is located two and a half miles down the Keese Mills Road from Paul Smiths Corners on the left.

The first Roman Catholic church in the town of Brighton was the Church of the Angel Gabriel, built in 1896. It served the needs of its parishioners until 2004 when it was closed by the Diocese of Ogdensburg. Its status for the future is uncertain.

Paul Smith donated the land for all the local churches. When asked by a guest why he did this even though he never went to church, he said that he did not care much for organized religion, but just in case he turned out to be wrong, he wanted to have his bases covered.

Two

EXPANSION AND SUDDEN DISASTER

The death of Lydia Smith led to son Phelps, above on the right about 1920, to follow in her footsteps as the business manager of family operations. He became his father's right hand, and together they led the company to further expansion.

from the trudeau family including the new daughter
that is to be & L. Trudeau   E. L. Trudeau

This 1912 Christmas card was sent by the family of Dr. Edward Livingston Trudeau. Trudeau, one of Paul Smith's oldest friends, was the founder of the Adirondack Cottage Sanatorium in Saranac Lake. He spent his life working to cure tuberculosis.

In the early 1900s, winter sports started to become more popular in the Adirondacks. Lake Placid was the first place to adopt them as a regular activity for guests. These people at Paul Smith's Hotel seems to be having a good time on their snowshoes.

This is the Keese Brothers water-powered sawmill about 1875. Later on it was sold to Patrick Ducey and incorporated into his lumber operations. In 1898, it was purchased by the Smiths. They installed a 150-kilowatt hydroelectric generating plant at the site and started the Paul Smith's Electric Light and Power Company.

The hydroelectric plant at Keese Mills was so successful that Paul Smith's new power company built three plants on the Saranac River at Union Falls, Franklin Falls, and Saranac Lake. This is the dynamo from the Union Falls plant.

In the early days of the electric power company, the Smiths also got into the electric appliance business as a way to expand the market for electricity. These are stacks of new refrigerators piled up in front of the Paul Smith's Electric Light and Power Company's headquarters in Saranac Lake. In 2009, this building houses Saranac Lake village offices on Main Street.

On August 1, 1896, the St. Regis Golf Club was organized. The 18-hole course was built on the site of the former Wilcox farm on the west end of Osgood Pond. The soil proved too sandy to grow good grass, so the course was moved in 1904.

This was the golf house built for the 1904 course near the new fairways south of the Keese Mills Road along the St. Regis River. Golf became a very popular activity in America at this time. Several Adirondack hotels followed Paul Smith's lead and constructed courses during this period.

Ben Muncil was a local designer and builder of great camps and other buildings in the area and around the eastern United States. In this 1920s picture, he shows how a fashionable golfer would be dressed on the links.

Muncil, right, had a hard and interesting life. He was one of 17 children of a shiftless Civil War veteran. He became a logger at 14, doing a man's work. This picture was taken shortly after he became a guide at 19. When one of his clients offered him a carpentry job at his camp, his true talent was discovered. By 30, he moved from carpentry to building design and started his own construction company.

In spite of years of trying, Muncil was never able to learn to read, but his daughter read correspondence courses on construction to him, and he remembered every word. He overcame what would today be recognized as a learning disability to build some of the most famous great camps in Adirondack history, including Topridge, White Pine Camp, and many others. Muncil was killed in a car-and-train collision in Gabriels in 1930.

Not all the hotel jobs were as exciting as leading hunting parties through the forest. This is how the lawn was mowed at the hotel in the days before gasoline-powered engines. It must have been a quieter job, but it did have its hazards.

This is Glover House about 1915. Built about 1892 as a rental property by the hotel company, Glover served as Pres. Calvin Coolidge's official office when he summered at Paul Smiths in 1926. It was later the home of several Paul Smith's College presidents and is one of the college buildings listed on the National Register of Historic Places.

In the early days of the 20th century, automobiles were playthings of the rich. The roads were not very good, but the more adventurous guests brought their cars on vacation. In response, the hotel turned one of its stables into the hotel garage. As seen by the busy attendants, it started to offer service for the cars also.

Paul Smith remained very active in his later years. Here he is horseback riding in 1905 at the age of 80. However, he developed a kidney problem in 1912. After treatment at several hospitals, he died in Montreal. He was 87 years old.

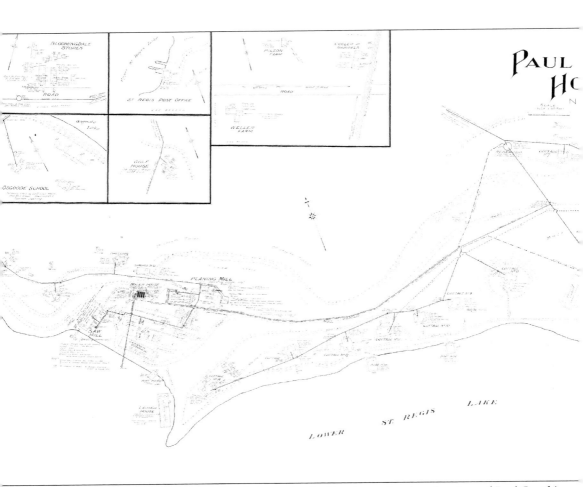

This 1914 map of Paul Smith's Hotel shows the facility that existed at the time of Paul Smith's death. He and Lydia Smith started out with a 17-room country inn and no one to do any of the

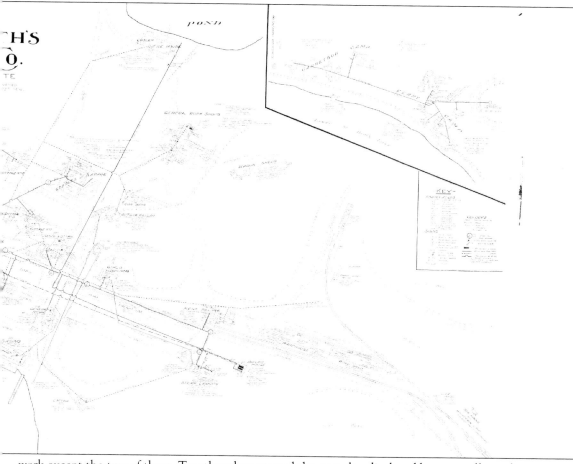

work except the two of them. Together they created the complex displayed here as well as other business interests throughout the Adirondacks and beyond.

In the early 1920s, cars began to become more commonplace. Here they share space with a horse and wagon in front of the main hotel building while guests enjoy the lakefront.

Lem Merrill's full name was Elmer Marcellus Merrill. He was a surveyor, and he knew the mountains as well as anyone alive. He was most noted for the cabin colony he ran on his 1,600 acres as well as for being one of the Adirondacks' earliest conservationists. Is this picture the return from a hunt or a rescue mission? History does not say.

It looks like New York governor Al Smith caught some fish. This 1926 picture was taken in back of the hotel store by the lakeshore. Smith later became the first Roman Catholic to run for president of the United States in 1928. He was defeated by Herbert Hoover.

The soldiers relaxing here are camped on the hotel grounds during the summer of 1926. They were part of the contingent assigned to guard Pres. Calvin Coolidge, who was summering in the area.

The nature of tourism in the Adirondack Park started to change in the 1920s. The change is evident with the predominance of cars in this 1925 postcard of the hotel. With the rise of the American middle class during the 1920s, more of those middle-class tourists came by car, and the rich started to come less often to the big hotels like Paul Smith's.

The State of New York started to build more and better roads into the park in response to the increase in automobile traffic. Roadside cabin colonies aimed at the new driving public sprang up to serve their needs. To respond to this new market, the hotel company built the Bluebird Cabins, pictured here about 1939, south of the main hotel complex on Lower St. Regis Lake.

Hotel guests watch a baseball game on the lawn next to the hotel about 1910. This ball field and the tennis courts beyond are the site of Essex, Franklin, and Clinton residence halls in 2009.

Secretary of commerce and future president Herbert Hoover (right) was among the many visitors who came to Paul Smith's Hotel to visit and conduct government business with Pres. Calvin Coolidge that summer.

Pres. Calvin Coolidge hated the hot, humid summers in Washington, D.C., and for the summer of 1926, he set up a summer White House at Paul Smiths. He stayed at White Pine Camp, a private great camp on Osgood Pond. Here Coolidge and his wife, Grace, and son John are playing with their pet white collies Rob Roy and Prudence Prim.

Coolidge descends the steps of Glover Cottage on the hotel grounds. Glover housed his office that summer. One of the roads on the hotel grounds passed by the back of Glover Cottage and gave a view right into the window of the room where Coolidge sat at his desk to work and receive guests. Viewing the president became such a popular sight for hotel guests that the Secret Service had to post a guard to keep an eye on who was back there.

One of Grace Coolidge's favorite activities was to walk the family dogs. Here she is on the White Pine Camp grounds. The owners of the camp brought in a forester from Europe to do tree work on the estate. The tree on her left shows evidence of his efforts in the brickwork incorporated into the tree.

The Pres. Calvin Coolidge liked to spend his spare time fishing. Here he is about to head out on Osgood Pond. According to the *Boston Sunday Post*, his favorite fishing guides were Edward Rork and Ed Corbin from the hotel guide staff.

Coolidge is on the left and Phelps Smith is on the right in front of Glover Cottage. By this time, Smith was totally in charge of all hotel company operations. Glover Cottage is on the National Register of Historic Places and is still in use by Paul Smith's College.

In addition to the Secret Service men protecting the president, there was also a contingent of Marine Corps guards. Here Coolidge is inspecting the Marine Corps camp. There were nearly 20 buildings on the grounds at White Pine Camp. These included the owner's cabin, where Coolidge stayed. His building had a bedroom, sitting room, dressing room, bath, and maid's quarters with a separate bedroom and bath. The U.S. Marines supplied their own accommodations.

This 1928 aerial photograph shows Paul Smith's Hotel at its greatest extent. The main hotel is in the center foreground, the Casino/boathouse is on the lake to the right, and the store is a little above and to the left of the Casino. The railroad tracks came in from the right in front of the three multistory buildings spread out in that direction.

On September 5, 1930, everything changed. A fire started in the electric wiring on the top floor toward the center of the main lodge. This wiring went back to the 1890s when electricity was first installed.

The closest fire department was in Saranac Lake, 12 miles away. It took almost an hour to answer the first alarm. By the time the first fire equipment arrived, the building was fully involved.

The fire was so intense that the firemen had to work in teams. One team used a mattress as a shield in order to get close enough to spray water on the fire while a second team hosed down the mattress to keep it wet enough to protect the others. Clouds of steam rose from the hot, wet mattresses.

The structure burned to the ground in four hours. None of the guests or employees were hurt even though this was before the days of fire alarms in hotels and most other public buildings. The credit goes to the two telephone operators who rang every room in the hotel while the building was on fire in order to warn everyone.

Three

DEPRESSION AND WAR IN THE ADIRONDACKS

Smith Cottage, which was an annex to the main building and home to the Smith family, was turned into the hotel and headquarters for the company. It was a much smaller building, but business had been declining throughout the 1920s.

C.C.C. CO. NO. 220-CAMP 12-N.Y. OCT. 1934, PAUL SM

9

The hotel fire of 1930 was just one more piece of bad economic news during the early years of the Great Depression. When Franklin Roosevelt became president, he inaugurated his New Deal to help Americans out of the Great Depression. On March 21, 1933, the Civilian Conservation

, CAPT. *Charles P. Eihlers* , COM'D'G.

Corps (CCC) was established as a jobs and training program for young men. By October 1934, a CCC camp was established on the shores of Osgood Pond in Paul Smiths.

The camp men were 18 to 25. They earned $30 per week, and $25 of that was sent home to their families. The conservation projects they worked on included reforestation, forest pest control, forest fire prevention and fighting, recreation development, and more. Gay Prue, Walt Stahl, and some friends are playing around in the snow at Paul Smiths. The men also had organized sports teams, crafts, and classes to occupy their spare time.

In August 1995, there was a reunion of CCC veterans at Paul Smiths for the dedication of a plaque marking the site of the camp. Among those in attendance are, from left to right, Clayton Winters, Leroy Smith, William Lytle, Paul Benoit, Elmer Charlesen, Walt Stahl, and Chuck Komeraski.

80

C.C.C. CO. NO.220-CAMP 12-N.Y. OCT. 1934, PAUL SMITH'S, N.Y., CAPT. *Charles P Elkhart* COM'D'G.

The Paul Smiths camp, like the other CCC camps, was not fancy, but it met the needs of the men. The camps were organized on the model of army camps and were run by U.S. Army officers. There was a mess hall, barracks buildings, toolsheds, workshops, and classrooms. The CCC ended in 1942 when World War II started and the eligible young men were drafted into the army.

Phelps Smith began to plan for the building of a modern, new hotel. His plan was to tear down the Casino and erect the new hotel on that site right on the water. However, he died in 1937, and all work ceased. In his will, he left the Paul Smith's Hotel Company and all its holdings to the founding of a college in his father's name on the site of the old hotel.

The new Paul Smith's College established by Phelps Smith's will was supposed to open in 1942. Instead, World War II started, and the hotel/college buildings were leased to the U.S. Army Signal Corps. Here Women's Army Corps (WAC) recruits receive training on rebuilding and repairing radios.

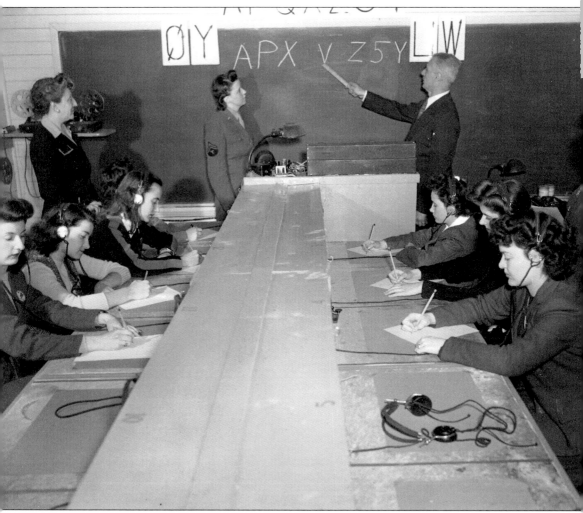

In this class, the WACs are learning how to transmit messages in secret codes. There were also classes of Signal Corps men who trained at Paul Smiths during this time but few pictures of them survive.

The WACs did not spend all their time in the classroom, even in wartime. Here they are on the third hole of the hotel golf course. In the background is the boarded-up golf house waiting for better times or the return of hotel guests.

When the war ended, the GI Bill made a free education possible to millions of returning veterans who would not have been able to even think of attending college before the conflict. In order to get ready for these returning veterans, the new Paul Smith's College had to repurpose the old hotel buildings. Those early students nicknamed this, one of the original college dormitories, "the Snakepit."

Other buildings that had been housing for summer hotel employees were also given over to residence halls for the students who were part of the first class to enter in the fall of 1946. This was the male workers' residence for the hotel.

Four

THE COLLEGE OF THE ADIRONDACKS

For the first few years, the facilities were makeshift. A snack bar, complete with jukebox for dancing, was set up on the lake side of the main floor of the old hotel store. Milk shakes were 20¢, hot dogs were 15¢, and hot fudge sundaes were a quarter.

There were so many veterans at the college that a U.S. Army Reserve unit, the 625th Forest Engineers Company, was established on campus. Pvt. Glenn Schmidt and Pvt. Jack Norton are operating an early version of the chain saw.

This is a group photograph of the 625th Forest Engineers taken in the college gymnasium in 1957. In the front row are William Rutherford (far right) and George Peroni (second from right), longtime faculty members in the forestry division. They had first met on the battlefield in Europe when they were frontline combat officers during the war. They never expected to meet again in the Adirondacks.

During the 19th-century heydays of Paul Smith's Hotel, hunting was always one of the most popular activities of the guests. After the college was founded, students kept up that tradition. In 1951, Ed Sudol poses with his buck after a successful day of hunting. The hunting tradition continues with many students in the 21st century.

When Phelps Smith left his estate to the founding of the college, he stipulated that one of the majors must be hotel and resort management. The programs offered in that area have evolved over the years, but one constant has always been courses that teach students how to prepare excellent food. These 1954 students are posing with the products of their final examination in the special foods class.

For many years, the biggest hotel convention in America was held in New York City. Hotel students were responsible for setting up and staffing a booth at the hotel show, advertising the college to attendees. In 1951, Don Reasor, John Paolone, and Robert Peck are on duty to answer questions about their college.

Students were also responsible for setting up exhibits for special events on campus. For this event in 1958, students put together their vision of the original rough country inn opened by Paul Smith in Loon Lake in the early 1850s, called Hunter's Home. It came complete with a representation of the first keg of rye whiskey Smith set up to serve his guests.

The air is full of sawdust as a forestry student runs a board through a planer. The hotel sawmill was changed from strictly a production facility to a teaching tool, where forestry students learned the art of sawmilling.

Just like in the old days, the logs were floated to the mill on Lower St. Regis Lake. Only this time the students were the ones who had to handle the various jobs under the eyes of faculty and the sawmill professionals. Jerry Pincoske is getting a log ready in 1962.

Howard Welch was the head sawyer for the hotel company and later for the college. Much of the lumber used in the new buildings constructed by the college in the 1950s and early 1960s was cut on college-owned land and milled in the college sawmill by Welch and the students.

Another major in the forestry division was and continues to be surveying. In 1989, Ellen Hooker learned to use an early version of a theodolite, a surveying instrument used for measuring angles, in one of her field classes.

Sometimes people forget that the full name of the school is Paul Smith's College of Arts and Sciences. Most of the early graduates and many today are liberal arts majors. They received their hands-on education through activities like participating in the play that the Drama Club is practicing here in 1959. Cindy Bates and Al Gates occupy center stage in this tense scene.

As with most colleges of that era, dances were an important part of everyone's social calendar. However, in the early days, there was a problem with dances at Paul Smith's College. Women often made up as little as 10 percent of the student population. In order to rectify this situation, the college bused women in from the predominantly female teacher's college at Plattsburgh. A busload of women is arriving from Plattsburgh State for the annual Paul Bunyan Dance in 1956.

Even the dances were different at Paul Smith's College. One of the features of every Paul Bunyan Dance was a woodsmen's team demonstration. The crowd is paying very close attention to this demonstration at the 1957 dance.

For residents of the Adirondack Mountains, one activity that is most available is skiing. Members of the 1953 Outing Club are posing on a campus hillside before they go out to hit the slopes.

An advantage that skiers had at Paul Smith's College was that the school owned its own ski slope on nearby Jenkins Mountain. The slope opened during the 1949–1950 school year, and student volunteers did most of the work of building it. The hill even included a 25-meter ski jump.

PAUL SMITH'S COLLEGE
JENKINS MOUNTAIN
SKI   AREA
PUBLIC   INVITED
1,000 FT TOW - WARMING HUT
SLOPES - TRAILS - JUMPS
SCHEDULED MEETS

Student sports were not limited to the outdoors. Practice for the 1953 basketball team was interrupted for the photo opportunity that resulted in this picture. In 1950, the college started to give athletic scholarships, and the records of its sports teams improved dramatically.

Wrestling was a popular sport on campus for many years. The 1963 team includes (first row) John Bower, John Cain, Harry Comins, and Ralph Strong; (second row) Bernie Wents, coach Ken Norton, Forest Corey, Barton Biondolillo, and William Bower.

Another of the liberal arts is music, but the 1957 college band attracted students from every major. The tradition of student musical presentations continues with the open mike nights put on by biology professor Dr. Curt Stager on Thursday nights in the Hutchins Café in the Joan Weill Adirondack Library.

Even though there were sometimes not many women enrolled at the college, they did dominate certain activities. In 1963, the cheerleading squad poses in the gymnasium. From the left to right are A. Clark, C. Shelter, C. Hudson, S. Keagle, J. Prentiss, L. Howe, P. Murphy, and E. Babb.

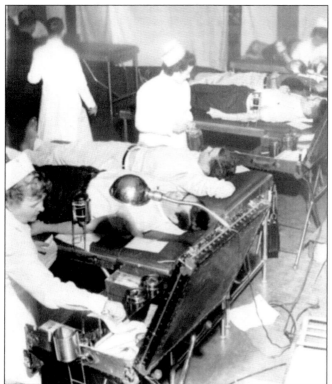

Community service has always been an important part of student life at Paul Smith's College. At this student-sponsored Red Cross bloodmobile in March 1959, 84 students gave blood, almost 25 percent of the student population.

After the snack bar moved out of the old hotel store, its new home was on the lakeshore. At most colleges, the place where students spend their leisure time is called the student union. At Paul Smith's College, it was the recreation hall, or as most students called it, the "rec hall." Here it is in the late 1960s.

The snack bar was a big draw for students in the recreation hall. In this 1955 picture, students are waiting in line for the chance to make an order at the snack bar soda fountain.

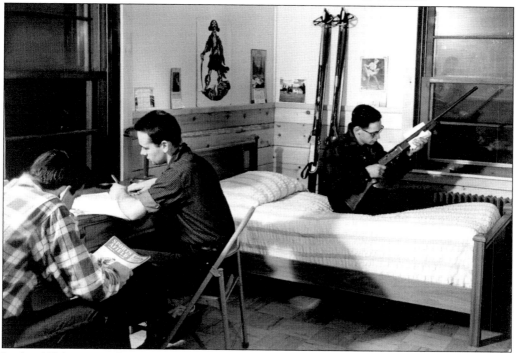

In this 1954 picture of a quiet evening in a men's dormitory, originally titled "Dorm Life," several elements of early college life can be found. A hunter cleans his gun in anticipation of a day in the woods while his roommate does his homework, and a fellow outdoorsman looks through a copy of *Sports Afield*. Note the now-antique skis leaning against the wall.

Not all dormitory rooms were as quiet as the previous picture. Here two students practice for an upcoming performance.

The styles and artifacts of the early 1960s are captured here, as two female students pose in their room in a girls' dormitory in 1963.

Cooler Hall was designed and built by the hotel company as a cold storage facility for meat in the days before electricity was invented. Water pipes ran from nearby Cooler Pond to gravity feed cold water through a system of pipes in the building. This kept the meat locker cold. During the college years, the first floor was the studio of the campus radio station, and the upstairs housed several students. It was torn down in 1982.

From 1946 to 1958, the second floor of old hotel store was the home of the college library. Geraldine Collins, the first college librarian, is helping students in the library on a snowy day in 1954.

The college maintained many traditions that came out of the hotel company. One of them was the annual Christmas party for the children of all employees and local residents. Harold Ryan stood in for Santa Claus in 1950.

This employee Halloween party was held at faculty member Gray Twombly's home in 1955. Twombly later became a dean and acting president.

The recreation hall was the largest space on campus in its early days, so it served as the main gathering place for important campus events. College president Dr. Chester Buxton is addressing an assembly of faculty and students in 1954.

By 1958, the main campus was beginning to look more like a college and less like a 19th-century hotel. In this view, a new dormitory, Clinton Hall, is in the foreground. The old hotel store is right behind it. Smith Cottage, to the left, was the only building still used to accommodate guests as Paul Smith's Hotel. The newly completed Frank L. Cubley Library sits on the lakeshore to the right.

Money was very tight for the new Paul Smith's College in the 1950s, so many of the early buildings were designed and built by the staff and faculty. Head carpenter Randolph Martin is overseeing the hoisting of the 76-foot trusses that will hold up the roof of the first college gymnasium in 1952.

Even the recreation hall was not big enough for some events. Graduations were held in nearby St. John's in the Wilderness Church. This one was held in 1954.

The stone walls of St. John's in the Wilderness Church made for a very regal background for graduation. In spite of those surroundings, Dean William Rutherford, front right, and Prof. John Huntley, center, did not find the speaker very exciting at the 1953 ceremony. However, Dr. H. G. Pickett has his eye on the camera.

For most of its history, the symbol of Paul Smith's College was the leaning pine. This early-1950s photograph shows the distinctive tree, with Smith Cottage in the background. When the pine was destroyed in 1971, tree ring dating put the year it began to grow at 1689.

Smith Cottage became the Paul Smith's Hotel. It was used as the college hotel and was a practical training ground for students in the various hotel- and restaurant-related programs.

On June 27, 1962, Smith Cottage was destroyed by fire. Plans had already been made to move the on-the-job training part of the hospitality curriculum to a larger, more modern facility. This fire hastened the transition.

The new home for the hospitality practicum was the Hotel Saranac on Main Street in Saranac Lake, shown here in the late 1960s. The Hotel Saranac was opened in 1927 as the only fireproof hotel in the Adirondacks.

These students are studying in the Pine Room of the Frank L. Cubley Library. It might look like an Adirondack mural on the wall to the left, but it is the view of St. Regis Mountain out the windows of this lakefront library.

One of the highlights of winter in the northern Adirondacks is the Saranac Lake Winter Carnival. Since it was begun in 1897 by the Pontiac Club, winter carnival has been promoting social and athletic events in mid-February ever since. The Saturday afternoon parade through the center of the village is the one event that brings everyone together.

Winter carnival brings all facets of the Saranac Lake community together. All the floats are homemade, and there are people of all ages and backgrounds participating in the parade and viewing it along the packed streets. These hockey players are trying to drum up support for an indoor arena in 1967. Their efforts were rewarded when the Saranac Lake Civic Center was built shortly after.

Paul Smith's College is very much a part of the Saranac Lake community, so it has taken part in the winter carnival parade for many years. This is the college float from 1965.

This float was a prizewinner in another parade in the early 1960s. Compare the lack of snow in this picture with the obvious and more normal subzero conditions on parade day that the young hockey players had to endure.

The college's location in the Adirondack Park has always been a draw to students interested in the outdoors. That made the Outing Club a popular organization for many years. The 1960 club members look like they are ready to go snowshoeing. Third from the left in the second row is Ted Mack. He returned to the college as librarian in 1969 and was the advisor to the Outing Club for many years in the 1980s and 1990s.

Another student organization with an interest in the outdoors was the Archery Club. There was an indoor archery range in the basement of the Buxton Gym Annex. The 1965 club is posing at its entrance.

Ruth Hoyt and Charlie Kirche are caught between classes in 1965. Hoyt taught for many years and went on to found the college museum. She worked tirelessly to preserve the historic heritage of the hotel days. Kirche started teaching math to U.S. Army Signal Corps trainees at Paul Smiths during World War II. He then taught at the college until his retirement.

Hollis "Red" Parsons was a fixture in the local community. His store on Easy Street was the closest place to campus to buy gasoline, beer, and other essentials. He was known to give more than one student a tank of gasoline on the cuff so they could get home for the holidays.

Enrollment grew through the 1950s and 1960s to the point that more student housing had to be built or acquired. The college purchased the former Gabriels Sanatorium from the Sisters of Mercy in August 1965. This is the entrance to what was then the Gabriels campus in 1970. The U.S. post office for the village of Gabriels is also shown. It marked the entrance until it burned in 1972. The gate was removed in 1976.

This 1979 aerial photograph shows the Gabriels campus of Paul Smith's College. The campus was used to house forestry students. The 100 acres of the former sanatorium was originally a gift to the Sisters of Mercy from Paul Smith in 1895.

This is Rest-a-While Cottage as seen in a 1920s postcard. The building was used by the Sisters of Mercy to house patients. After the facility was purchased by the college, the building was converted into a residence hall.

The college started a sugar bush in 1946. The sugarhouse in this 1976 photograph was built in 1950 and improved upon over the years. The forestry division still offers students a course in sugar bush management, and the maple syrup is sold in the college store.

Baker House was built in 1896 as a rental building for Paul Smith's Hotel. It was used to house female students when the college opened in 1946 and then as a residence hall until the early 1980s. After being closed for many years, it was remodeled with a gift from trustee Ralph Blum. In 1999, the lakefront building was reopened as Blum House for honor student housing.

One of the most successful teams at Paul Smith's College has always been the woodsmen's team. The team competes in timber sports like sawing, ax throwing, fire building, and tree felling. Most team members are drawn from the Forestry Club. This is the 1967–1968 club posing in front of the fireplace in the Forestry Club cabin.

The pulp toss is one of the events in every timber sports meet. In this event, students toss 4-foot-long pieces of timber between two stakes 20 feet away. In 2001, Brett McLeod, in the gray sweatshirt, watches Dave Teter compete in Montreal, Quebec, for the men's A team.

There are men's and women's woodsmen's teams, as well as events for mixed teams of men and women. These are called jack-and-jill events. This is jack-and-jill crosscut sawing from Montreal, Quebec, in 2001. On the saw are Matt Charland and Rose Thelen. The women holding the log are Amanda Brenemen, left, and Mary-Kate Helm.

With wood chips flying in his face, Matt Barkalow competes in the crosscut sawing event. The fastest competitor to saw through his log wins.

Ax throwing at a target can be one of the more spectacular events in timber sports. During practice in the late 1970s, the members of the woodsmen's teams are watching one of their members throw his ax at a target.

Forestry professor Gould Hoyt was the coach of the woodsmen's teams for more than 30 years. In this picture, he is demonstrating proper felling technique to an audience near the hotel store. Behind him is Herb "Stumpy Jr." Seaman. When this former woodsmen's team member died shortly after graduating, a stained-glass window was purchased for the Forestry Club cabin in his honor.

"Be something special, be a chef!"
Culinary Arts – Fall, 1995
Paul Smith's College of Arts & Sciences

By the 1990s, one of the largest programs at the college was culinary arts. Students and faculty posed for this publicity picture in 1995.

Spring can come late to the northern Adirondacks. In 1966, students and faculty are cutting ice and sluicing it over the spillway dam on the St. Regis River off Keese Mills Road so they can get some open water in order to practice canoeing.

In the winter of 1966, students are leaving Longtin Cafeteria after lunch. Longtin served as the largest dining hall on campus until it was destroyed by arson on October 20, 1995.

At the time of the fire, Longtin was the only dining hall on campus. In one of the great feats of community organization and spirit, employees and students worked around the clock to convert the main gymnasium into a dining facility. Food was prepared by the culinary arts faculty and students in their teaching kitchens until new kitchens could be rebuilt.

The last original 1869 Paul Smith's Hotel Company stagecoach sat in storage for over 60 years. In 1987, a group of employees and retirees decided to resurrect it as one of the last links to the hotel days. Through volunteer work and donations, the coach was restored and is now used for special occasions like this one in 2007.

The outdoor classroom on the hill behind Cantwell Hall is usually occupied by students whenever the sun shines. A recreation class is in session here in 2007.

The Joan Weill Adirondack Library opened in January 2002. The building has become the physical and intellectual crossroads of the campus because it combines library services, information technology, and other academic support services under one roof. The library has always welcomed the general public to use the facility in the center of campus.

Every program has courses where students take part in experiential learning. Two students in the Culinary Arts Department, Dustyn Ford and Danielle Fuller, are working on a baking project in 2008.

In February 2005, a student in the arboriculture and landscape management program is taking part in an arboriculture class. Students in this class are trained in the practical aspects of arboriculture, including how to properly climb trees without spikes in order to prune them. In the background is the Freer Science Building. (Courtesy of Prof. Randall Swanson.)

Electrofishing is a technique that students use to conduct population density studies in the fish and wildlife program. Aaron Stredny and Krystle Olszewski are working on a project in the Smitty Creek research area near campus.

Another part of the massive remaking of the campus that has taken place in the 21st century is the Joan Weill Student Center. It contains a lakeside dining hall, student life offices, a bookstore, a culinary arts student restaurant, and other facilities. The center opened in 2006.

The spirit of community service continues to be a part of student life. In the spring of 2007, Paul Smith's College students joined others from across America to take part in Step It Up. This movement to stop global warming was started by former college trustee Bill McKibben.

Paul Smith's College students enjoy the same views of Lower St. Regis Lake and St. Regis Mountain that guests at Paul Smith's Hotel enjoyed 150 years ago. Future generations of students will continue to be able to take advantage of the educational opportunities now available at this treasured, historic location.

BIBLIOGRAPHY

Collins, Geraldine. *The Brighton Story: Being the History of Paul Smiths, Gabriels and Rainbow Lake*. Lakemont, NY: North Country Books, 1977.

———. "Paul Smith." *Franklin Historical Review* (1965): 4–11.

DeSormo, Maitland C. *The Heydays of the Adirondacks*. Saranac Lake, NY: Adirondack Yesteryears, 1974.

Donaldson, Alfred L. *A History of the Adirondacks*. New York: Century Company, 1921.

Kudish, Michael. *Historical Update: Paul Smith's College Lands, Forests, and Buildings 1981–2004*. Paul Smiths, NY: Paul Smith's College, 2004.

———. *Paul Smiths Flora II: Additional Vascular Plants—Bryophytes (Mosses and Liverworts)—Soils and Vegetation—Local Forest History*. Paul Smiths, NY: Paul Smith's College, 1981.

Surprenant, Neil. "Ben Muncil: Builder of Great Camps." *Adirondac* (July 1986): 20–24.

———. "The Great Camp No One Knows." *Adirondac* (May 1989): 21–23.

———. "Paul Smith." *Adirondack Life* (July–August 1979): 19–21.

Woods, James R. *Paul Smith's College 1937–1980: A Saga of Strife, Struggle and Success*. Paul Smiths, NY: Paul Smith's College, 1980.

Discover Thousands of Local History Books
Featuring Millions of Vintage Images

Arcadia Publishing, the leading local history publisher in the United States, is committed to making history accessible and meaningful through publishing books that celebrate and preserve the heritage of America's people and places.

Find more books like this at
www.arcadiapublishing.com

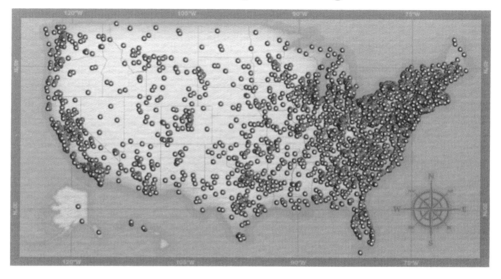

Search for your hometown history, your old stomping grounds, and even your favorite sports team.